The Good & Bad About Hard Money Lenders

SEAN T. DANLEY

Copyright © 2018 Sean T. Danley

ALL RIGHTS RESERVED. This book contains material protected under International and Federal Copyright Laws and Treaties. Any unauthorized reprint or use of this material is prohibited. No part of this book may be reproduced or transmitted in any form or by any means, electronic or mechanical, including photocopying, recording, or by any information storage and retrieval system without express written permission from Sean T. Danley.

ISBN: 9781728760919

10 9 8 7 6 5 4 3 2 1

www.405homebuyers.com

PUBLISHERS NOTE
Some names have been changed.

If you purchased this book without a cover you should be aware that this book is stolen property.

The scanning, uploading, and distribution of this book via the Internet or any other means without the permission of the publisher is illegal and punishable by law. Please purchase only authorized electronic editions and do not participate in or encourage electronic piracy of copyrighted materials. Your support of others' rights is appreciated.

TABLE OF CONTENTS

PREFACE

HARD MONEY MEANS TO AN END

HARD MONEY PROBATE HOUSE

THEY FLIPPED THE HARD MONEY SCRIPT

HARD MONEY MOTHA*%&AS!!!

HARD MONEY MADE SIMPLE

HARD MONEY QUESTIONS

ABOUT THE AUTHOR

Sean T. Danley

PREFACE

Like many people in this day and age, I often feel as if I suffer from information saturation. With information so readily available and accessible at the click of a mouse, screen swipe or voice command, I remind my kids how *easy* their lives are. My spiel often begins with, *Long before Wikipedia*…electronic books and cell phone apps, I anxiously awaited the days when a new set of encyclopedias were due to arrive in the mail, weighing in at about twenty pounds, mind you; just to see what new information had been printed in the latest edition. And no, I didn't get new encyclopedias every year—I wasn't that fortunate. I remember a time when I had to physically go to the Inglewood Library, rifle through index cards to jot the location of a book down with pencil and paper, search three floors to locate the actual book, stand in the checkout line, take the book home to read, and return it to the library—all before accruing any late fees. Whew, it sounds like work compared what todays youth are accustomed to.

There was a time when I had to use the single, big black dictionary we had in the house to find word definitions. A time when I had to pull over to the side of the road and skim through that thick, wire bound, Rand-McNally Road Atlas to drive from point A to point B if I didn't know where I was going. A time when I had to browse through the weekly TV guide just so I'd know what time I needed to plant myself in front of the "idiot box," as my dad used to call it, to catch one of my favorite TV shows. There was no on-demand, on-screen guide, and definitely no DVR that allowed you to watch at your leisure and fast forward through commercials.

My how times have changed, and despite the plethora of self-help and business books, blogs and vlogs available to the masses, I chose to write this series of quick read, real estate investment e-books to provide you with information on how to avoid some of the mistakes and pitfalls I've encountered throughout my journey as a real estate investor and landlord. After all, mistakes should be hailed as valuable lessons that teach us what *not* to do in the future. Hey, I've made plenty of mistakes, so hopefully you won't have to!

Whether the reader of this first installment of my *Good & Bad* books, be a newbie or seasoned real estate investor, a first-time homebuyer or seller, I hope that you'll at least find that one "ah ha" piece of information that you might not have heard before. Or perhaps you'll come across that question you'd never thought to ask before choosing a hard money lender. Either way, I hope the information I've decided to share will make you a better investor going forward.

HARD MONEY MEANS TO AN END

Let's just clear up one of the biggest lies ever told in the real estate investment world right off the bat. *Hard money loans are for people with bad credit.* This is absolutely false! Only those who have never utilized its power believe the stigma associated with hard money loans. In fact, hard money is probably used by some pretty smart and savvy investors. I linked-up with a local real estate broker to help locate prospective investment properties. At the time I was working full-time as an Investigator for the Oklahoma Real Estate Commission, which required me to investigate complaints filed against real estate licensees, alleging everything from minor advertising violations to fraud and embezzlement. After ten years of doing that, I had a tough time placing trust in real estate agents. It's ironic, because I had been a real estate agent prior to becoming a regulator, so I knew they weren't all bad. But my job put me face-to-face with the good, the bad, and the ugly side of the real estate industry. Worst of all—the incompetent! The real estate industry demands a level of competency in law and regulations, due diligence, attention to detail, positive social interaction and business acumen. Some practitioners often demonstrate this lack thereof.

Being an Investigator often put me in an awkward position, since I always felt this weird apprehension from people I wanted to do business with outside of work. I mean, I'm a consumer too, and I did actually take my Investigator's cap off at 4:30 or 5:00 p.m. everyday. Still, I think some of the people privy to my job title assumed that I was on some sort of covert mission to catch them breaking real estate laws. But actually, nothing was farther from the truth.

The broker I decided to work with was an older, white haired gentleman named Daniel who had been in the business about 30 years. His name had never come across my desk at work, which was a good thing. I even researched whether or not he had any complaint history pre-dating my time at the Commission, and luckily he didn't. He ran a one man shop; no big name franchise or a bunch of associates under his supervision. But he did own the two story commercial building that housed his office and about 14 other small businesses. You see, Daniel was an investor like me, so I knew he understood the mindset and motivation of an investor, or so I thought. For true investors, there is little, if any emotion involved in the investment—just numbers.

Don't get me wrong, Daniel worked out as an agent despite a few snarky political remarks. I mean this guy literally asked me what my party affiliation was during our first meeting. When I told him I was a Democrat he facetiously said, "I won't hold it against you." I really didn't care that he was a Republican, but he could have kept his party affiliation and political opinions to himself. As the Obama era came to a close and the unapologetic, politically incorrect rhetoric of Trump began its ascent, I think every Republican felt the need to let anyone who would listen, know which side of the aisle they stood on. My goal was to do business with him and nothing more. Besides, opinions are like assholes—everybody has one and most are full of shit! I think Daniel was intrigued that I was an Investigator with the Commission. He had some political connections and sat on a few real estate industry committees in the past.

With his help, I purchased two properties; the first was a short-sale listed on the MLS that I planned to renovate and flip; and the second was real estate (REO) or bank-owned property that I planned to rehab and hold as a rental. I purchased both properties using hard money loans, but structured completely differently, which I'll get to later. But in a casual conversation with Daniel during the showing of another prospective purchase, he warned that I **"stay away from the hard money loans"** and go with conventional bank financing at 5, 10 or 20% down.

At the time, he was in the process of selling his office building, which coincidentally houses my real estate office today. In a prior conversation he mentioned that his older brother was independently wealthy, so the first thing that popped into my head when he cautioned me about hard money loans was that I didn't know a single, independently wealthy individual. And I certainly didn't have a rich brother I could bum a cool five to ten grand from, but I understood his point. It left me wondering just how much he knew about hard money loans other than the stigma associated with them that most likely stems from the seemingly high fees and points lenders charge.

Hard money loans should be a means to an end, and not the end game. If utilized correctly, hard money can be a wonderful tool for picking up distressed properties very quickly. As an investor you want to use other people's money (OPM) as much as possible, and I've used hard money over and over again to minimize the money that comes out of my pocket on just about every single real estate deal—but not every deal. I'll explain that later. I warn that all hard money lenders are not created equal, so your due diligence is crucial before engaging a hard money lender. I'll walk you through four separate experiences I've had with three different hard money lenders. You'll come to understand the differences between the three, and hopefully wipe away some of the stigma you may be harboring about hard money already.

Sean T. Danley

HARD MONEY PROBATE HOUSE

My younger brother relocated from California to Guthrie, Oklahoma to attend Langston University in 2006. Coincidentally, my wife's grandmother was raised in Guthrie and later settled in Oklahoma City. She was battling breast cancer when we arrived. Both of them had already suggested that we relocate from the overcrowded, overpriced, hustle and bustle of Los Angeles to OKC.

My short-lived real estate sales career in Los Angeles tanked along with the real estate market meltdown of '07. My wife got laid off from her marketing job at a West Hollywood firm while still pregnant with our second child. Times were tough, so "what the hell" we thought. The move to OKC might do us some good, so we packed-up a couple of months after our daughter was born and made the trek halfway across the country with our two babies in tow. With what little savings we had, we prayed that it would all work out once we got settled.

My wife's grandmother was a retired school teacher, and years earlier her middle son had convinced her to buy some rental properties. She took his advice and purchased five single family homes that she could leave to each one of her five children upon her death. She allowed me and my wife to reside in one of those properties, rent free until we got on our feet. Most of her grandmother's properties were tiny, wood frame houses built around the 1900's, with some deferred maintenance issues. To boot, they weren't in the most desirable neighborhoods. I worried mostly about my wife because our new living quarter was a huge downgrade from what we were both accustomed to. But, the place was free and we appreciated her grandmother for providing a roof over our heads.

In the popular 70's sitcom *The Jefferson's,* the theme song goes, *"…Movin' on uhup…"* But the look on my wife's face when she first laid eyes on that old house was more like, *"…Movin' on doowwn…"* And in that moment, I knew I had to get us outta that place *quick!* Nowadays, I jokingly sing the lyrics, "...*Movin' on doowwn*..." to remind my wife about the look on her face that day. We count our blessings today and look back and laugh about those tougher times.

We were both able to find work soon after arriving to town. About four months later, my wife's great, great uncle, J.D., whom she had never met, passed away. He died a widower, without a will or any living children, so my wife's grandmother (his niece) began the probate process. She was named executor of his estate and because of my real estate experience and job as a Real Estate Investigator, she asked me to take a look at her deceased uncle's house. Coincidentally, J.D.'s house was just about a mile and a half west of our shabby, little digs. But that slight distance made a world of difference.

I pulled up to the overgrown lawn of J.D.'s 1973 ranch style house located in the quiet, diverse, working-class neighborhood, known as The Village. I had already searched the Oklahoma County Assessor's website to find that it was a 1700 square foot house with four bedrooms and two baths. I opened the front door and swore I was back in the 70's. From the pink bathroom tile, wood paneling, and green carpet, to the linoleum floors, everything was original, outdated décor. And because J.D. had been admitted to the hospital before passing, roaches, as they often do, had made themselves right at home in his kitchen cupboards. Still, it was a great house with good bones as I like to say—a place I could definitely call home, after a serious cosmetic overhaul, of course.

I decided to buy it and suggested to the probate attorney that we conduct a probate sale that didn't require court confirmation. That just meant the process of the estate selling the property would be much less restrictive and complex. But how would I buy it? I had been on my job for about six months and my credit was crap! My plan was to use a local hard money lender that advertised at real estate investor meetings I'd been attending. OKC was a goldmine for investing. Real estate here appreciated at a normal pace and not outrageously like many coastal cities around the country. Plus, the cost of living was great. I later came to realize that many investors from California owned rental property in Oklahoma City, Lawton and Tulsa. Why? Because it was still affordable and you could certainly cash-flow.

I'd offer the estate a fair price, and within six months I'd be able to refinance the house as a permanent residence. You see, hard money lenders don't care about your exit strategy, be it sale or refinance, so long as you have one that results in paying them back their money. Now, before you decide that hard money lending should be your alternative to FHA, VA, or conventional home financing, let me stop you by saying it is not.

Hard money lenders typically only lend to entities like an LLC (limited liability company) or corporation formed for the purpose of investing, and not making the property a personal residence. In fact, most hard money mortgages include an attestation that indicates you the investor, will not reside in the subject property. Further, hard money costs are exorbitant as compared to typical consumer mortgages, so you wouldn't want a 30 year hard money loan, nor would you be able to find one.

The hard money lender I engaged to purchase the probate house was called Red Land Lending, and like most other hard money lenders they would lend up to 70% of the ARV or after repair value. I started the process of performing my due diligence, which involved researching the county assessor's website and locating some recent sales comparables; these are the most recent sold properties in close proximity to the subject property. They should always be similar in size with the same number of bedrooms and baths.

I determined that J.D.'s house had an ARV of about $125,000 and needed about $25,000 worth of work, which I didn't have. What I did have was free rent, which couldn't have come at a better time. The money I would have otherwise been paying for rent, I could apply toward monthly interest payments to Red Land.

The deal was too sweet to let get away, so I had to make it work. My experience in the real estate industry allowed me to talk the talk, even if my credit and bank account couldn't walk the walk. I applied with Red Land hoping they'd base their decision to lend on my experience, job, and of course, J.D.'s property that I could buy for about sixty cents on the dollar. I offered the estate $72,000, which my wife's grandmother accepted. To substantiate my offer price, I provided the probate attorney pictures and a rehab budget detailing what I planned to do to bring the property up to full market value. After that, the probate attorney began the process of identifying and notifying all of J.D.'s heirs about the sale. The majority lived out of state and probably had no real personal relationship with him, but that's how the probate process works. It's not every day that people are notified by mail that they're entitled to a cut of a long lost relative's estate, so there was no opposition to the sale.

Turns out that Red Land liked the deal and was willing to lend, despite my credit shortcomings. If the numbers work, most hard money lenders will fund the deal, although each one establishes its own approval criteria. I had to send the following information to Red Land before they'd analyze the deal:

- Property Address
- Copy of LLC Documents including Operating agreement
- Fully executed purchase contract, with LLC as the Purchaser
- Insurance and Agent Info. with premium paid or to be paid at closing
- Title company information
- Buyer's Real Estate Agent Info
- Retail Improvement Sheet or Repair Detail
- Exit strategy
- Brief list of experience
- Last 2 years tax returns
- Financial Statement on the principal of your company

The required documents can vary from lender to lender, but be prepared to provide most if not all of the items above. Red Land had no minimum FICO score requirement, but in subsequent years I've seen many hard money lenders impose minimum FICO score requirements of about 600. Red Land's loan terms and fees looked like this:

- LTV (loan-to-value): Up to 70%
- Loan Term: 6 months;
- Interest Rate: 12-15%
- Annual Interest Rate: 12-15%
- Points: 4-5
- Pre-Payment Penalty: None
- Property Analysis Fee: $500
- Credit Application Fee: $250
- Pre-Payment Penalty: None
- 6 mos. Interest paid monthly
- 6 mos. Insurance Pre-Paid at closing

Remember when I mentioned earlier that my ultimate goal was to refinance J.D.'s house and live there? Well, I didn't exactly tell Red Land that tidbit of information. I just let them know that I'd be selling or refinancing once the work was done. Again, I don't suggest you get into the habit of using hard-money to finance your future personal residence, although I have heard stories of some house flippers who make a habit of moving into their flips immediately after the rehab. They reside in them for six to twelve months and then sell. In my opinion, that's more relocating than I'd like to drag my family through time and time again.

I closed on J.D.'s house about three weeks after getting final approval from the probate attorney, and the only money I shelled out was the $750 I paid Red Land for their property analysis and credit application fee. I also had to take about $900 to closing to pay the property insurance premium for an entire year. Earlier I mentioned that all hard money lenders are not created equal. Well, Red Land required proof that the premium was either paid-in-full, at or before closing. In subsequent deals with other hard money lenders, I had the option of paying the premium in monthly or semi-annual installments. If you choose to pay the premium in full and end up selling the property in less than six months, any unused portion will be refunded to you. Be sure to ask your insurance company about their various payment options. No need to shell out money on a full premium if you plan to sell within a few months.

Because I was new to town, I didn't have any contractor connections and Angie's List was not a household name at the time. Luckily, my brother's boss was also a real estate investor who did rehab work in his spare time. In fact, he had sold my brother one of his own flip projects. With no were else to turn, I relied on my brother's connection to help me complete most of the work. I also intended to put in some sweat equity of my own to save some money.

Back in California, I was raised around the building trades. Before becoming a real estate agent, my dad had been a Journeyman Electrician. And his younger brother (my late uncle) had been a Journeyman Plumber, so as a kid I'd do side jobs with either of them some weekends. Although I wasn't ever fond of hard work, I could tolerate it, so as the real estate market began to look bleak, I took a job as a Service Tech with Roto Rooter. Hell, I had bills to pay and a family to support. And although my time there was short-lived, the plumbing skillset I gained was invaluable; so much so that I've been able to save thousands of dollars in plumbing repairs, I would have otherwise paid out to some other plumber.

For about a month and a half, my brother's boss and his crew of two to three guys would work their day jobs, and from about 6pm to just after midnight they'd work on my rehab project; most weekends too. Every step of the way, I was right there helping and soaking up everything I didn't already know about the rehab process. They call it *sweat equity* for a reason, because I'd put in eight hours at my day job, go home to grab a quick dinner, change clothes and head straight to my flip to work until after midnight. I did this Monday – Friday without fail and put in another six or seven hours a day on the weekends. It wore me out, but I was younger then and destined to get that house done before Thanksgiving. Without my wife's support I would have never been able to get that project done, because she'd work all day too and go home to care for our son and daughter who were both under four years old at the time.

I had a handshake deal with my brother's boss, which I don't recommend under any circumstance. It's best to put any and all business agreements in writing. The work they did was great, but there were days when they'd put my project on-hold to take on some other small, quick paying side job. Some nights, I'd be there alone, working tirelessly to get the job done. And other nights and weekends, my brother would lend a hand to the project. I was grateful to him as well. The crew agreed to be paid when I got a draw check from the lender, which meant they had to complete a certain amount of work in order to be paid, and then move onto the next phase.

Understand that most, if not all hard money lenders charge inspection draw fees ranging anywhere from $150 to $250. After verifying the progress on your rehab, the inspector prepares a report with photographs that is then submitted to the lender. Only after they approve the completed repairs will they issue a draw check, either by bank wire or paper check. Some lenders withhold the inspection fee from your draw, while others require you to pay the inspector directly out of your own pocket at the time of inspection. I've done both.

When you schedule your inspections, make sure the actual work you're requesting to be reimbursed for has been completed—not in the process of being completed, halfway completed, or just about completed, but complete! For example, if you're asking to be reimbursed for the new HVAC System installation, which can be one of the more costly rehab items, don't let the inspector show up to find the air handler and blower have been installed, but the condenser hasn't. Why? Because most lenders will consider that incomplete and they will not issue you a check until it's 100% complete. Sometimes, you may get away with it, depending on the inspector. If not, you've wasted $150 to $250 bucks on an inspection that you thought would result in a fat draw check being cut. It makes you look unprofessional and left having to explain to your contractors why you can't pay them for the work they've done—all because you called for an inspection too soon.

Each hard money lender has its own repair improvement budget they refer to for repair draws. Some are simple, while other are much more detailed.

1. Paint:	Interior $_____	Exterior $_____
2. Flooring:	Carpet $_____	Tile/Vinyl $_____
3. Plumbing:	Kitchen $_____	Bath $_____
4. Electrical:	Exterior $_____	Interior $_____
5. Doors:	Exterior $_____	Interior $_____
6. Windows:	Replace $_____	Repair $_____
7. Other:	Pest $_____	Debris $_____
8. Landscape $_____		
9. Permits $_____		

The list above is an example of a fairly simple repair improvement budget that I use with my current hard money lender, who I'll talk about later. It's short, sweet, and not in the least bit complicated. I like less complicated, but the next example was a more detailed and lengthy spreadsheet used by Red Land, as you'll see:

	Borrower Company Name / Point Person:	
	Property Address:	
Date of Original Estimate:		
Purchase Price:		$65,000
Number of Bedrooms (Proposed):		3
Number of Bathrooms (Proposed):		1.5
Above Ground Finished Square Feet (Current):		1261
Above Ground Finished Square Feet (Proposed):		1261
Below Ground Finished Square Feet (Current):		0
Below Ground Finished Square Feet (Proposed):		0
Labor & Materials		**Budget Entered By Buyer**
Project Prep Work, Demolition, Abatement, Plans, Permits		**$ 1,000.00**
Demolition, Roll-offs, Dump Fees, and Clean-Up Fees		$ 1,000.00
Architect / Engineering Plans		$ -
Building Permits		$ -
Property Survey		$ -
Termite Treatment		$ -
Mold Abatement		$ -
Asbestos / Lead Based Paint Abatement		$ -
Pest / Animal Abatement		$ -
Exterior Items		**$ 3,470.00**
Foundation / Structural		$ -
Roof - Replacement		$ -
Roof - Patching		$ -
Roof - Ice Dam Removal		$ -
Roof - Soffit Vents		$ 20.00
Gutters / Downspouts		$ 250.00
Chimney		$ -
Siding		$ -
Masonry / Concrete Work		$ 600.00
Shutters		$ 150.00
Exterior Paint - Home Only		$ 1,800.00
Exterior Paint - Garage / Outbuilding Only		$ -
Deck / Porch / Patio		$ -
Driveway / Walkways / Misc. Concrete Work		$ -
Garage - General		$ -
Garage - Siding		$ -
Garage - Roof		$ -
Garage Doors		$ -
Garage Door Motors / Opener		$ 400.00

43	Garage Door Motors / Opener	$	400.00
44	Grading / Dirt work	$	-
45	Trees, Bushes, Plants, Misc. Landscaping	$	200.00
46	Dead Tree Removal	$	-
47	Fencing	$	-
48	Sewer Line / Private Well	$	-
49	Mailbox	$	50.00
50	**Interior Prep Work, Framing, Windows, Insulation, Sheetrock**	**$ 3,900.00**	
51	Framing	$	-
52	Trusses	$	-
53	Insulation	$	-
54	Stairs	$	-
55	Railings	$	-
56	Windows	$	500.00
57	Egress Windows	$	-
58	Skylights	$	-
59	Fireplace	$	500.00
60	Sheetrock - New / Repair / Patching	$	500.00
61	Sheetrock - Tape / Mud	$	-
62	Sheetrock - Retexture Ceiling / Walls	$	1,000.00
63	Install Trim / Base / Door or Window Molding / Crown Molding	$	400.00
64	Stain Wood	$	-
65	Enamel Wood	$	-
66	Interior Paint	$	1,000.00
67	**Mechanical Systems: HVAC / Electrical / Plumbing**	**$ 4,890.00**	
68	Air Conditioning	$	150.00
69	Furnace	$	2,500.00
70	Clean and Certify Furnace	$	-
71	Duct Cleaning	$	-
72	Electrical Rough-In	$	250.00
73	Light Fixtures	$	400.00
74	Ceiling Fans	$	-
75	Exterior Security Lights	$	100.00
76	Switch Plate Covers	$	30.00
77	Smoke / CO2 Detectors	$	60.00
78	CATV / Phone / Stereo Pre-wiring	$	-
79	Electrical Final	$	250.00
80	Plumbing Rough-In	$	400.00
81	Plumbing Fixtures	$	500.00
82	Washer / Dryer Hookups	$	-
83	Appliance - Washer / Dryer	$	-
84	Hot Water Heater	$	-
85	Sump Pump	$	-
86	Plumbing Trim / Final	$	250.00
87	**Flooring and Doors**	**$ 1,450.00**	

Regardless of the form required by the hard money lender, be sure to complete the work you're asking to be reimbursed for, before calling for an inspection. I repeated this because I can't stress the point enough. I had to learn this lesson the hard way when I thought I could get away with my floors being some 80% complete at the time of inspection. I think I even remember telling the inspector that they'd be finished in the next day or two. Well, to my dismay, it was a no-go and I didn't receive the draw amount I was anticipating.

I think I was short some $1500 bucks because the floors were almost done! If you happen to find yourself in such a predicament, hopefully you will have a very understanding contractor who can wait to be paid until the next draw (highly unlikely), or you'll have to pay the contractor out of your own pocket (most likely). Just know that you'll be the one waiting to recoup those funds from the next draw.

Whenever I go into a rehab project using hard money, I try to limit my draw requests to three or four, tops! Remember, inspections cost you $150 to $250 a pop, so a few of those can easily add $500 to $1000 to your rehab budget. Try to get as much work done as possible and then call for inspection. This, of course will depend on your cash reserves going into the project.

I don't care how many guru's you listen to that preach flipping houses with no money can be done—I ain't buying it! And I've bought and rehabbed over a dozen properties. Not once, did I do a deal that cost me zero dollars, although there were times where my out-of-pocket expense was minimal. On this first probate flip, my interest only payments came to about $1050.00 a month, but I also had to cover the cost of utilities; gas, water and electric every month. You should be prepared to pay deposits to initiate each of these services, which can sometimes cost about $200 each.

Some contractors may ask for a deposit to get started, but I don't recommend you get into that habit. Why? Because there isn't a single job that pays people before they do work. Why is a contractor any different? When I first started, I had no money to pay contractors up front, but I could foot the bill for materials they needed to get started. Within a week-and-a-half or two weeks, a portion of the work was done, so I'd call for an inspection, and pay them as soon as the wire hit my bank account. Now, as a more seasoned investor, I don't like to go into any rehab project without at least $10,000 in my bank account. That way I'm not worried about any delays or issues with paying my contractors.

Earlier I suggested you put your agreements in writing. That's because, toward the end of this probate flip, I ran into a minor dispute with my brother's boss about his final payment, which he stated would be under $5000. Well, I gave him $4500 as final payment, but he disputed the amount, saying that we had agreed on $5000. I didn't have a problem paying him $5000, had we actually agreed on that price, but he understood "under $5000" to be $5000, and I understood it to be

$4500, which is under $5000. We had nothing in writing to prove either of our positions, so he begrudgingly accepted the $4500 as final payment. But I think that experience taught both of us a very valuable lesson; a verbal contract is about as good as the paper it's written on. Get it in writing people!

    My wife's grandmother lost her battle with breast cancer before she got to see the finished house. I remember her being so excited that we'd have a nice home to live in. In December, we moved into the probate flip, and the smile on my wife's face was a stark contrast to that frown she wore in front of her grandma's rent house eight months earlier. Now, I had to figure out how to refinance the place. Right around March of the following year, I found a local mortgage broker named Valerie, who gave me the raw and uncut news about my credit; it wasn't good enough to refinance the house. I had a bunch of lingering little collection accounts I needed to rectify. Instead of kicking me out of her office, Valerie gave me a play-by-play rundown on how to restore my credit. But, in the meantime I had to sell the house.

    I asked Red Land to extend my hard money loan to 12 months, so that I could get the property sold. They obliged to the tune of another $2500 fee that had to be paid up front. You see, the initial 3% loan fee was rolled into the loan, so I didn't have to come out of pocket at first. But now that I needed an extension, they stuck it to me! Or should I say, I stuck it to myself. I borrowed the $2500 from my dad with the promise that I'd pay him back after it sold. I paid Red Land's extension fee and listed the house for sale with one of Valerie's business associates. Her name was Lena, and like Valerie both of these women would become valuable industry resources I would turn to in the future.

    In hindsight, my exit strategy should have been rock solid before I attempted to purchase the probate property, but it was a lesson well learned. Whether you choose to rehab and flip (sell) or rehab and hold rentals, I urge you to establish a relationship with a lender that has pre-qualified you and is willing refinance your properties once renovated.

    Lena quickly secured a buyer for the probate flip, but that buyer's inspection revealed that the roof needed replacing, so she backed out of the deal. Luckily, my insurance covered the entire replacement cost and a second buyer came along, happy to know that she was getting a fully renovated property with a brand new roof.

I walked away from the closing table with a check for just over $10,000; mind you, I had to pay my dad back the $2500 he let me borrow to extend my loan. Hardly a profit based on the nine months of interest I paid, but still it was money back in my pocket and several invaluable lessons I could take into the next deal.

THEY FLIPPED THE HARD MONEY SCRIPT

I took break from real estate investing to focus on my job, repairing my credit, and purchasing another home for my family. I was able to get just about every one of those collections settled and removed from my credit report, which eventually raised my credit score to over 720. A few years later I was ready to jump back into the investment game, but this time with a solid plan in place. With Valerie's help, I pulled some equity out of my primary residence; some of which I planned to use to jumpstart my real estate investing business. This was about the same time I began working with the proud, Republican, Real Estate Broker, Daniel. Lena was my first choice, but she was mostly a listing agent who preferred working with sellers. Daniel set me up to receive automated MLS listings that matched my desired property criteria, and every day I searched those listings religiously looking for deals.

After a week or so, I came across a short sale listing that had pretty much gone unnoticed for a few months, which was odd in a market where turnover was pretty rapid. Perhaps other investors didn't see its value or just didn't want to waste time on the short sale process, which can be lengthy. It was a 3 bedroom/2 bath house that needed a full cosmetic makeover. The owners were headed to foreclosure if they didn't get it sold soon.

I recognized the home's value immediately, located just outside of The Village, where I'd flipped the probate house. I had Daniel prepare an offer and I came to realize that the listing broker just so happened to be the brother of the owner of Red Land. Yep, it's a small world after all, and one thing I learned after moving to OKC is that this small, Midwestern town is home to some family dynasty's that have accumulated millions, even billions of dollars across a number of industries. If you don't know the story of oil tycoon J. Paul Getty, his father, George Getty, was an attorney turned oilman who struck it rich when some land he owned in Bartlesville, Oklahoma began cranking out black gold (oil) in the early 1900's. So for the heir apparent, J. Paul Getty, it was only natural that he end up with "All the Money in the World" with the kind of head start he had. This of course doesn't take away from his own business acumen that he used to grow his family's fortune exponentially.

After performing my due diligence on the short sale property, I figured the rehab would cost me about $25,000, and I could easily flip it for about $125,000. My offer of $65,000 was accepted by the seller, although it took about a month for the mortgagee to give final approval. When dealing with short sale properties the lender/mortgagee is agreeing to take a loss on the mortgage balance, so they alone make the final decision to accept or reject purchase offers. It simply depends on just how much of a loss they can tolerate. Still, a short sale saves them the added legal expenses and drawn out timeframes associated with the alternative foreclosure process.

I went back to old, faithful Red Land to finance this deal. Only this time their terms had changed a bit. Yep, they flipped the script on me and every other investor they did business with, for that matter. Instead of paying interest over a six month period like I had before, they required investors to pre-pay the entire six-months interest at closing. Ouch! Perhaps they had taken on too much risk in the past, but whatever the reason for this drastic policy change, it was gonna cost me about $7500 up front to get into the deal. Still, I couldn't let it get away—so what the hell? The numbers worked and I had the $7500 to take to closing. Also, if I sold the house at a profit before six months, they'd owe me a refund for the overpayment.

If I hadn't had the full $7500 to pay Red Land up front, I would have lost the deal. These are the moments that can make or break an investor, so do your due diligence when choosing a hard money lender. I believe it's best to be pre-qualified before you ever find a deal, so that that you're ready to pull the trigger when a deal finally comes your way.

I'd been keeping up with the real estate market by attending local investor meetings and reading articles on Biggerpockets.com regularly. I couldn't just sit by idly while waiting for the seller's mortgage company to wrap up the short sale, so I began looking for my next deal, which I stumbled across by searching the website of Oklahoma

City's premier REO (real estate owned) agent; Mildred Banner. I intended to buy a property I could renovate and hold as a Section 8 rental. My job with the Real Estate Commission kept me in constant contact with brokers and agents across the state, so I knew who the players were, and better yet, which bad actors to avoid. Mildred had to be at least 70 years old when we first met, but this little old lady had built a powerhouse real estate business. She'd call me at the Commission from time-to-time if she had a regulatory question or two. Don't get me wrong, Mildred was no bad actor, but because she ran a pretty big real estate outfit, she was also a big target for individuals looking to stir up an allegation or two.

Years earlier, while I was still a newbie real estate agent, I attended Saturday morning investor meetings at the Southwest Los Angeles Board of Realtors office. The meetings were led by a seasoned mortgage broker/investor named Freddie Burton, who made his millions in real estate. He'd written and self-published a book that I still reference today called, "From a Plain Coon to a Tycoon." In his teachings, Freddie talked about how much he despised poverty; even called for an all-out war against it. It was kind of an oxymoron, because he amassed much of his wealth by buying income property that he'd rent to low-income/poor tenants whose rents were mostly subsidized by the government. "If I serve the poor, I will eat with the rich," he'd say. Freddie's blueprint set the stage for me once I began investing. Unfortunately, he passed away in 2015 and I remembered him professing during our Saturday morning investor meetings that he would *control his money from the grave*. Freddie stressed the importance of estate planning often, so I'm sure that even from his grave he maintained a firm grip on his fortune.

I had about $15,000 set aside to invest, so I made a phone call to Donatella, who ran one of OKC's investor groups. I asked if she knew of a hard money lender that financed rental properties. She recommended a local guy named Jack that I'd seen around a couple of meetings before. His family had been in the Oklahoma insurance business since the early 1900's. They also loaned money to real estate investors, so I did my research and learned through public records that his company had funded hundreds of deals. In fact, a local investor with a sizable rental portfolio had used Jack to fund dozens of his deals. It was all the information I needed to at least give Jack a call.

Jack and I spoke at length about my plans and he sounded excited to take me on as a new client. But, I needed to know what he could actually do for me. Unlike Red Land, Jack lent money to investors who were looking to build rental portfolios. He offered a 10-year fixed rate mortgage at 10% and would fund up to 70% of ARV. However, he didn't provide repair funds, which meant if the property needed repairs, you'd have to foot the bill yourself or buy it for less than 70 cents on the dollar. Although there was no hard and fast requirement, Jack stated that he wanted the borrower in the deal for two years before refinancing or selling the property. If you chose to hold onto his financing, the property would be fully paid for free and clear after ten years. He asked for the usual financial documents much like Red Land, and so long as the value was there and a clear title, Jack could close in as little as a week and a half.

Mildred's REO listing was a 3 bedroom, 2 bath brick home built in 1979, with good bones, located in a somewhat newer subdivision of Spencer, Oklahoma. It did need some work; at least enough to pass a Section 8 inspection, but it wouldn't be as simple as that. You see, banks weren't just giving away their REO inventory. They'd already taken a hit on the foreclosure, so the list price was right at about 70% of ARV. And because I was using Jack to finance the deal, I'd have to pay for the rehab out of pocket, which I estimated to be right around $10,000.

I had Daniel draft an offer of $42,500, which the bank accepted. I turned-over the transaction documents to Jack and met him at the house while he performed his appraisal. The next day he called and said we were good to go. His process was much simpler than Red Land's. In fact, his appraisal came in a little higher than I expected, so the loan covered the purchase price and all closing costs. I didn't have to take a dime to the closing table. In fact, I walked away from closing with a $500.00 check. Trust me, you'll grow to love deals like that. The only money I spent prior to closing was an earnest money deposit of $1000.00, which the seller/bank required, and a $500 fee that Jack charged for credit review and appraisal. What appealed to me about Jack's hard money loan program was that he didn't charge the typical 3-5 points per loan that most hard money lenders do; just a simple $200 loan fee that was rolled into the loan.

I should probably stress that when dealing with REO inventory, you're typically at the mercy of the bank/seller. They like to use their own contracts and often remove inspection contingencies, but I'd still suggest you go through the property with a contractor if you can. Don't expect to receive a property condition disclosure statement either. Banks are exempt from disclosure, but hey, if your plan is to renovate the property, just make sure you and your contractor know what needs to be done. Banks also like to dictate where closing will take place. Nine times out of ten it will be some closing company in another state, but they'll coordinate with a local closing agent where you'll be able to sign closing documents.

Financing with Jack naturally sounded like a sweet deal on the surface, but remember I had a 10% APR, which brought my note to about $575.00 a month. This figure included principal and interest amortized over the ten year term of the loan. It didn't include taxes or insurance. HUD establishes fair market rents that you can research online for most states and cities throughout the country. You can also obtain this information from your local Section 8 office, and it's updated annually. For the rent house in Spencer, Section 8 would pay up to $850, but that wouldn't be until after I renovated it and located a suitable tenant with a subsidized housing voucher. Then, the house would have to pass a Section 8 inspection, otherwise known as Housing Quality Standards.

I knew the place would be vacant for at least a couple months, so I'd be shelling out principal, interest and insurance payments with zero return in the interim. Unless you have a loan with PITI (principal, interest, taxes and insurance) combined, property taxes have to be paid twice a year in December (1st half) and April (2nd half). Hard money lenders require insurance and taxes to be paid, but not held in escrow.

The rehab took just over a month and I recruited my brother and 12 year old son to help demo and replace the vinyl floor tiles. I paid them of course, and hired a painter and a handyman to do the rest of the work with everyone working evenings and weekends to get it done. I secured a tenant as soon as I put the house on the market and Section 8 approved the property within a few weeks. By month three I was cash-flowing.

The monthly math looked something like this:

+ $850.00 Rent	
− $575.00 Principal and interest	
− $73.00 Insurance	
− $65.00 Tenant Gas Bill	
= $137.00 Net Income pre-tax	

As good as this deal looked on the front end, it wasn't as colorful on the back end, and the net income didn't leave much room for repairs or taxes. Turns out, that old 10% monthly interest was killing my profits. No offense to Jack, because I'd gotten into the deal because of him, but over the long term, his hard money was costing me way too much. As soon as I had a signed lease in hand, I refinanced the property out of Jack's 10% mortgage and into one with a local bank at 5.5% over 15 years. That refi made my numbers look like this:

+ $850.00 Rent	
− $344.00 Principal and interest	
− $73.00 Insurance	
− $65.00 Tenant Gas Bill	
= $368.00 Net Income pre-tax	

As you can see, I added $231 a month to my net pre-tax income after refinancing the property. I also walked away from the closing table with a check for $10,000; thus recouping my out-of-pocket rehab expenses.

The short sale deal I'd been waiting on closed during the tail end of the Section 8 rental rehab, and even though I had to cough up just over $7000 in pre-paid interest, it was a little satisfying to know that I didn't have a monthly note to pay; especially while I was already paying the note and footing the entire rehab bill on my unoccupied rental. Be sure to always know your budgets and timelines. This is especially crucial if you intend to take on more than one project at a time. Hard money can be a great tool if used properly to your advantage, or it can potentially hurt your deals.

I had to fire the original contractor I hired for the short sale flip. He started dragging his feet toward the end of the project, which was going to push my timeline way over the anticipated deadline. We parted ways and I found a couple of other guys to finish the bath and shower tile and floors. If you're wondering why I haven't gone in-depth about the rehab process itself, it's because this book is about hard money and not flipping houses. If you want a superb book to read about flipping houses from A-Z, I highly recommend, "The Book on Flipping Houses" by J. Scott. I've read a lot of real estate flipping books, but none of them comes close to being as thorough as J. Scotts.

Unfortunately, I didn't read his book until after my first three rehabs, but I still managed to walk away with a check for $32,000 just four months after purchasing the short sale property. And yes, Red Land refunded about two months' worth of that interest that I'd paid up-front.

HARD MONEY MOTHA*%&AS!!!

Once you get a few successful deals under your belt, it puts you in a pretty good head space. Your confidence is high and it makes you eager to go after more deals. At least that was the case for me. My brother was already holding onto an inactive real estate sales license, so as my short sale flip project was nearing completion, I suggested he activate his license and I'd let him list the property. He'd put a few grand in his pocket, and then he could help me find more deals.

My brother took my advice, so I parted ways with Daniel to help my brother further his real estate sales career. I was looking to add another Section 8 rental to my portfolio, so my brother helped me find a bank-owned property not too far from the short sale flip. However, it was in another zip code; a C/D class neighborhood, which made it the right house to add to my Section 8 portfolio. It needed a full interior and exterior cosmetic rehab, but like my other rental, it too had good bones.

The property just so happened to be listed by Lena, who had sold my probate flip a few years earlier. Like Mildred Banner, Lena also kept a steady inventory of REO properties. As for financing this new rental, I could have gone to the local bank I used to refinance my other rental, but they required 25% down. Lena was asking $40,000 for the place and I estimated repair costs to be about $15,000. I was coming off of the short sale flip, so I certainly had 25% to put down, but the old real estate adage that tells investors to use other people's money (OPM) was stuck in my head.

Besides, there was enough equity in this place for me to buy and rehab with only paying the mortgage interest. Once I could secure a tenant, I would immediately refinance with my local bank. All they needed was an executed lease.

During the renovation of my first rental property, I hired a handyman who prided himself on being a Navy Veteran and SeaBee. He did good work, so I also wanted him to do some of the work on this new rental project. If you've never heard the term SeaBee before, don't worry, I hadn't either. These men and women are also known as the Naval Construction Force (NCF). For my own peace of mind and to verify what this SeaBee thing was about, I put a call into one of my cousin's that had also served in the Navy. He confirmed that SeaBees can build entire towns if necessary. They're highly skilled workers that eliminate the need for the Navy to hire civilian construction companies. It was all the confirmation I needed.

Since I knew which contractors I'd be hiring, I decided that my best method of financing would be to go back to Red Land. Remember, I was trying to use as little of my own money as possible, despite the fact that I had it. I had my brother draft the offer, but before he sent it over he said Lena wanted a $4000 deposit; an amount equal to 10% of the asking price. Now, I won't say that this amount was customary or even a requirement of the bank, because I'd put a $1000 deposit on Mildred's REO listing. Still, I found myself at the mercy of the bank.

In my professional opinion, the 10% deposit was required to eliminate any would be wholesalers trying to flip a contract with no ability or money to close on their own. Or perhaps it was Lena's attempt to simply protect the interest of her client, the bank. I couldn't fault her either way, because I knew there was value in the property, so I wrote a check and had my brother deliver the four grand to the title company.

I then sent the transaction documents to Red Land for review, complete with their long, drawn out rehab budget and detail sheet. I waited a few days for them to complete their appraisal, certain that they'd come back ready to roll. To my dismay, instead of approving my loan, they sent me a letter that read the following:

Due to lender inspections & underwriting the property does not qualify for a loan based on the following: requested purchase price of $40,000. Therefore, we are unable to offer funding on this property. If you have any questions,....

Yada, yada, yada…"These hard money mothaf*%&as!!!!," I thought to myself. My heart just about sank to the floor because I had put up a $4,000 earnest money deposit that I was not about to walk away from. I called the office and got some lame explanation about their valuation being lower than mine, and their rehab estimates being more than mine. This is precisely why you must know your numbers, in addition to the lender's full criteria. Turns out, Red Land's inspector estimated repairs to be roughly $30,000; double my $15,000 budget, which sent my LTV (loan-to-value) ratio through the roof. My mistake was trying to save a few dollars by using a hard money lender that primarily lent money for flip projects, and not rehab-to-rent deals. Red Land's inspector came up with a budget geared toward a retail flip, but I was simply looking to make the property Section 8 rent-ready. Even after explaining my intentions and contesting their inspector's $30,000 budget, Red Land wouldn't budge or adjust their figures, so my deal was dead in the water!

With $4000 on the line, that's not how I saw it though! I had to resuscitate my deal and make it work—fast. I was contractually obligated to buy the property or else lose my earnest deposit. As soon as I hung up the phone with Red Land, I called Jack. He didn't really care how the place was gonna be fixed up because he wasn't lending repair money. He didn't need to review a repair budget. Hell, if I had kept the place vacant for the next ten years, so long as he got his 10% principal and interest every month, he'd be okay. I submitted the paperwork to Jack and within a couple days I was approved, and one step closer to closing.

Unfortunately, due to the course of events that transpired with Red Land, a serious monkey wrench had been thrown into my little plan to save money. I ended up having to pay for the entire rehab out of pocket…again. Ouch!!! That wasn't the plan, but I had the money, so rolled with it. Needless to say, I never did business with Red Land again. The fact that they wanted to dictate the cost of *my* rehab with no consideration for my own figures, left me disgusted with them. Was I to put granite countertops and bamboo flooring in a house I planned to rent to a Section 8 tenant? I think not, so I said to hell with them and their inflated budget.

Thanks to Jack, I closed on the deal and completed renovations in about six weeks. I secured another Section 8 tenant and took the deal to my local bank to refinance and maximize my cash flow. The figures on this house were initially identical to my other rental. Unfortunately, Jack didn't take too kindly to me refinancing out of two deals so quickly, despite the fact that he was paid back in full. He told me these weren't bridge loans and he wouldn't lend to me a third time. It was the first time I'd ever had someone upset about me paying them back in full. Are you just as confused as I was?

Well, a few months later I read an interesting book called "The Banker's Code" by George Antone. This is another highly suggested read for real estate investors; new or seasoned. Not until I read Antone's book, did I come to understand Jack's perspective and reasoning for not wanting to lend to me again. Jack was a banker who ran a private (hard money) bank, wherein he borrows money from private investors to invest in cash flowing notes backed or collateralized by real estate. He promises his investors a guaranteed return of 10% annually for at least two years—hopefully a full ten. Antone's book helped me realize that Jack's investors were expecting a 20% return over two years, which is better than any savings account or CD. So, when I turned around and refinanced out of those deals within a few months, his investors were essentially left with dead money (money that's not making any money). That is, until Jack finds a new cash flowing note backed by real estate.

As a result of this one deal, two bridges were burned, and at my age, I avoid burning bridges at all costs. One was my doing and the other was Red Land's fault. The only one that still doesn't sit well with me is the burgeoning business relationship I had with Jack. I can honestly chalk it up to my own ignorance about banking, but I'll forever be grateful to him for funding those two early deals.

HARD MONEY MADE SIMPLE

When you're ready to scale your real estate business, you should try to have two to three lenders you can turn to for funding your deals. My late Grandma Doris use to always say, "Don't put all your eggs in one basket." Those words couldn't have spoken more volume than in that final deal with Red Land that almost cost me four grand. I was lucky to have Jack on standby at the time, but I began to branch out and look for other lenders I could work with.

I requested a meeting with an older gentleman named Von that had been a guest speaker at a local Millionaire Possibilities meeting. He was a banker for another small bank near my home. We sat down in the bank's conference room and exchanged a bit of history about ourselves. I explained my investment goals and how I had used hard money in the past to fund my initial purchases and rehabs. I planned to continue doing so, and hoped that his bank could be another possible resource for refinancing my properties.

Von seemed genuinely impressed with me, and said he was willing to look at any future deals I presented. However, he cautioned that his bank was just getting into the single-family home investment sector, as they dealt mostly with larger commercial deals. These new smaller deals could take longer to process and they'd take a backseat to their customary deals. Before we ended our meeting, Von suggested I call a hard money lender based in Kansas City, Missouri that he'd known for many years. He thought I might like the lender's terms more so than Red Land's. He even said that I might find their process much simpler.

I never did get to work with Von, as he retired a few months after our meeting, but I did reach out to his hard money contact. I'm a person who tends to conduct some form of research online before I pick up the phone, so I reviewed the lender's website and found their rates and terms much the same as Red Land's. They also required many of the same documents from prospective borrowers. But, what they didn't require was six-months pre-paid interest. Nor did they have a $50,000 minimum loan requirement, which Red Land had implemented. I prepared a series of questions to ask the lender that would help me determine whether or not their program was truly different or just more of the same.

I called and spoke with Grant, the founder and president of the company. He was a retired attorney that had been in the hard money business for ten years. He said that he pretty much ran a one-man show and could lend up to 70% of ARV, but to determine value he always ordered drive by appraisals done by licensed appraisers. The real value in Grant's program was that if there was enough wiggle room in a deal, the investor could roll the full interest, closing and rehab costs into the loan, so long as those combined costs didn't exceed 70%. Even better, he didn't dictate to the investor what work needed to be done, or require the project to meet some minimum quality standard. So long as the work was complete as outlined in his repair detail form, he'd cut a draw check. He mentioned that a few of his clients would sometimes sit on their purchases for a few months without doing a single repair, and then turn around a sell at a profit.

Just from that conversation, I knew Grant was the right hard money lender for me. He came down from Kansas to meet me at our first closing and it was nice to put a face with a voice and name. We went on to do several deals and when he came to town, if I had a rehab going on, he'd stop by to personally deliver the draw check. In fact, as I write this book, I am a week away from closing on another recently completed flip project that was financed by Grant.

If you should be so lucky to find a hard money lender that makes the process simple, stick with them, so that you'll make your life as a real estate investor a little more simple…but just a tad. When you see hard money lenders advertising their services, it shouldn't be a red flag or deterrent that you avoid like the plague. Take the time to fully understand the lender's terms, so that you can make an informed decision. Know what you're getting into (HML terms), and know how you're getting out of the deal (exit strategy).

Certainly there are better alternatives to hard money loans, like private money; perhaps from people you know with hefty 401K's or self-directed IRA's. Perhaps your dad has a cool $1 million or should I say $64 million to lend you like so-called "self-made" billionaire Donald Trump! Hey, who needs hard money when dear, old dad can write you a seven or eight figure check? Hey, I don't believe people should make apologies for their success, but when these trust-fund babies dismiss nepotism and their silver spoons as being major factors in their success, I take issue with it!

Small, local banks like the one I use to refinance my rentals are good sources as well, but you'll have to do your research as well. Most of them will extend commercial financing to investors, and at today's interest rates they average about 5.5 – 6% amortized over 15 years. Most of them don't charge excessive fees or points like hard money lenders either, but be prepared to put 20-25% down on each deal.

Hard money has worked in my favor several times over, with a few bumps along the way. Hopefully, it will work in your favor too. If you're a new investor that chooses to use hard money along your real estate investing journey, ask other local investors for referrals; preferably HML's they've actually done business with, so that you're not led astray. Today, I get inundated with emails and mailers from hard money lenders from all over the country. Since the real estate market has rebounded from the 2007 debacle, many hard money lenders have come out of the woodwork. Do your due diligence and avoid getting stuck doing business with some fly-by-night operation that's here today and gone tomorrow.

HARD MONEY QUESTIONS

The following is a list of questions I wish I'd asked before I approached my first hard money lender that just may benefit you when approaching prospective HML's:

Do you have a minimum loan amount?

Housing costs vary across the county. For instance, I can buy a home in some parts of Oklahoma City for as little as $10,000 with an ARV of $40,000 - $50,000. You'll want to know before you waste any time, whether or not the HML will fund such a deal. It's not worth it to some HML's to deal with loans under a certain dollar amount.

How much skin in the game do I need?

You'll want to know if the lender requires you to have some actual cash in the deal before you move forward.

Do you have a minimum FICO Score requirement?

Most HML's have websites nowadays, so this requirement may be spelled out, but if not, it's best to know where you stand and what the lender requires up-front.

Do you withhold inspection fees or do I pay out of pocket?

Like I mentioned earlier, the lender may ask you to pay their inspector directly or withhold the fee from your draw proceeds.

Do you use an in-house appraiser or hire a licensed appraiser?

Because HML's lend money to businesses, rarely are they regulated by any government agency, but they will employ or contract with someone they deem competent and experienced enough to determine property values. Grant is the only HML, I've seen use an actual licensed appraiser to determine value.

Do you dictate the standard of repairs I have to make?

This is a big one that almost cost me a $4000 loss. Ask your HML up front, whether they simply rely on your renovation plans and budget, or do they impose some minimum renovation standard.

Does my investment portion have to be held in escrow?

If you should have to put money into the deal, will the HML require you to remit that money to them to be held in escrow? I took a meeting with a HML once and this was their practice. They required investors to turn over their 10-20% investment, which was then applied to the renovations over the course of the rehab. I never did use that company.

Are there any specific geographic areas that you do not lend?

I once found a potential Section 8 rental on OKC's NW side in another C/D neighborhood. It was bank owned and needed some work so I'd get Grant to finance the purchase and rehab, and afterward I'd refinance. Well, Grant denied the loan after I sent him the address. Turns out he had lent money to another investor on a project right down the street from this place, and when the investor couldn't sell or refinance it, Grant had to foreclose and take the property back. It was a bad experience and he didn't want to be put in that predicament again. I had to respect his reasoning, because he knew the area. It's kinda funny, because Grant later sold me that house he'd foreclosed on in a contract-for-deed deal. I held it for several months, and later sold it.

Also, Red Land once told me they didn't lend in Spencer, Oklahoma where I ended up owning a couple rentals, because they had to take back a couple of properties from investors that couldn't sell there as well.

My advice is to know your market and your exit strategy. Don't try to flip in an area where inventory doesn't sell fast. If you do, make sure you're qualified to refinance into a permanent loan, so that you can get out of your HML.

Do I need real estate experience?

It certainly helps to have some experience, and some HML's will require some sort of track record before they lend to you; but not all of them. It doesn't hurt to ask, but don't be surprised if a HML asks you for a brief biography along with your other documentation.

Do I need cash reserves?

When I got started I had no cash reserves; just an ability to pay. But since that time, I've come across several HML's that want to see verifiable cash reserves by way of bank statements; sometimes equating to 30% of your loan amount. Don't waste your time with those HML's if you don't have the money. There are plenty others out there.

ABOUT THE AUTHOR

Sean T. Danley was born in Los Angeles, California and raised in South Central LA and Inglewood. He studied at San Diego State University and later earned a Bachelor of Information Technology Degree from American Intercontinental University. His father, an electrician turned real estate broker introduced him to the real estate industry, and Sean became a Realtist® and Realtor®. He relocated his family to Oklahoma City in 2008. While simultaneously building a real estate investment business in OKC, Sean served as an Investigator and later Chief Investigator for the Oklahoma Real Estate Commission. Today, he continues to be an active real estate investor throughout Oklahoma County.

Sean can be reached at 405homebuyers@gmail.com.